Off Highway 20:

And Selected Poems

Dennis R. Bourret

Published by SurealWorks,
Tucson, Arizona 2016
www.surealworks.com

Published in the United States of America.

Library of Congress Control Number: 2016956780

ISBN: 978-0-9962610-1-2
ISBN: 0-9962610-1-X

Cover art: Echo Glen Bourret

Book design, cover and author photograph:
CreaytoStudios

To my "Gramma Peg"

who raised me for the first six years
of my life; taught me about initiative
and striving to achieve; instilled
compassion in me; and introduced
me to the printed word.

CONTENTS

Selelcted Poems

CONTENTS

THE CUP OF LIFE (Revisited)

Such vessels we are -------
Filled to the brim with our life's stories
And our emotions and thoughts
Are a mix of powerful brew.

Ultimately though, we develop cracks
From which our memories leak
Until there is little left
But residue.

Then we fall to the ground
To shatter into pieces
And be trodden underfoot
By a succeeding generation's shoe.

And our writings are but the shards
Of who we were
And only we know
If our lives were true.

OFF HIGHWAY 20

"O little town of yesteryear,
How still I see thee lie,
The hopes and fears,
And yes, some tears
I see in my mind's eye.
Each building's story
Brings me back.
I can tell them if I try."

Oh, little town
I sing your song
In hushed nostalgic tone.
I walk your streets,
All four of them,
And see time's damage done.

Far back in years
I roamed your streets.
My memory kept a log.
I knew the people
On every block
And every friendly dog.

I knew each house
And who lived there,
And whether they liked kids.
I knew each tree,
And who had swings,
And who's cookie jars had lids.

Then we moved,
My mom and I,
When Dad came back from war.
We went away
To start a new life,
And to follow ambition's star.

I grew up.
And became a man,
And fought in my own war.
I then came back
To connect again
And erase my spirit's mar.

What I found
Was what I'd heard
From friends I happened to meet.
The town had died,
And I then quietly cried,
As I wandered from street to street.

But then I knew
As I saw each house
That my memory was kind.
Each story lived
And the town survived
In the reaches of my mind.

THE GENERAL STORE

There it stands
At Main Street's center
The township's General Store,
The red brick building
With display-front windows
And a big wide swinging door.

There was a time
When it was the hub
Of this town's business space.
Farmers came
From all around
And shopped at a bustling pace.

Wives had sent
Their grocery lists,
Good food on which they thrived –
Gloves for work
And irrigator's boots
Straw hats and pocket knives.

A cold drink cooler
A big lunch meat slicer,
A cash register cranked by hand,
Vegetable tins
Stacked high on shelves
Were available on demand.

Farmers talked
About dollars per bushel
Or the sugar beet company's man.
Women looked
At reels of ribbon
And for flats of fruit to can.

The proprietor ran
The whole place by herself.
She was widowed when she was young.
She only got
Some occasional help.
From her car-wreck crippled son.

Her only daughter
Who was my mother
Was teaching in other towns.
My first six years
Were spent right here
In an apartment on the grounds.

I ate and slept
And played with my friends
And used the outdoor John.
I had a dog
And helped in the store
And built play forts on the lawn.

Now it's closed,
It's a store no more.
My grandmother's passed away.
The town is dying,
And folk don't come
For goods and needs of the day.

The postal clerk
Has bought the place
And uses one side only.
The few that come
To stop for their mail
Can sense the place is lonely.

THE LIVING QUARTERS OUT BACK

Way in the back
By the walk-in-cooler
We lived behind a door.
The living quarters
For the sake of convenience
Were attached to the back of the store.

A living room,
Two bedrooms, kitchen,
A room for Great-Granddad,
There surely was
For the four of us
Enough living space to be had.

I took my baths
In an old wash tub
In the middle of the kitchen floor
Until the time
A plumber was hired
To put a shower just outside the door.

Grandma and I
Slept in one bedroom.
My Uncle Bob got the other,
At least until
He went and got married,
And his wife became a mother.

Great Granddad
Came from Denmark.
He homesteaded but lost his land.
Then my grandma
Had his room built on.
With no choice but to lend a hand.

Grandmas are special
And mine was no different.
Her home was home for us all.
She ran the store,
And kept up the house,
And for family was always on call.

She'd be working
Out front in the store
But would come back along the way.
She'd make sure
I was up, dressed, and fed,
And was ready to meet the day.

Then, at noon,
She would dash back in
And stand at the stove and cook.
She did double duty
To take care of us all,
And would do whatever it took.

When I got older
She decided it was time
To show me how to whittle.
A pocket knife
And a fruit box slat
Said I was no longer little.

A little later then
With a bar between two trees
She challenged – "Hand walk its length."
The offer of a quarter
And a summer time to try
Started building my grown-up strength.

The most special times
Came some Friday nights
Since she knew my deepest wish.
We'd go to the lake,
Cook our dinner on a fire,
And stay until I caught a fish.

With Grandma's help
I got a start on my life
With these little things and more.
My first home
And my first family
I enjoyed in the back of the store.

The post office clerk
Lives back there now,
And goes about his way.
The chances are he isn't aware
Of the good things of yesterday.

THE TWIN BUILDINGS

Straight over
From the front of the store
Across the street on a line,
Two buildings stood
So close to each other
They seemed to intertwine.

They were owned
By the same old man,
But one had been shut down.
It had been
A millinery shop
Where a woman could buy a gown.

I remember
Once being asked
If I'd care to look inside.
I did and saw
A tin covered ceiling
And shelving long and wide.

Clothing racks
And lady's hat boxes
With dust over all I could see.
But as I looked
Then I could imagine
All the finery that used to be.

Its twin building
Was a little strange
As are buildings built in pairs.
It was a home
Used as a post office
Where people lived upstairs.

What I remember
Was my Uncle Bob
And what his job would entail.
He had a contract
To go meet the train
And each day bring back the mail.

Every morning
He'd go down to the station
Driving Grandma's old '36 Ford,
And I could go too
Just to pick up the mail
And ride on the car's running board.

The millinery shop
Has been torn down
And the post office is just a house,
But that old building
Now doesn't seem complete
Like an old man without his spouse.

THE IRON WORKS

..ie street
..ia down just a bit
A very large structure stood.
It was two stories high
With big sliding doors
And a sign made out of wood.

In days gone by,
If metal work was needed,
People came from far and near.
Be it tin-work
Or heavy arc-welding
They could always get in done here.

The Iron Works owner
Was a very smart man,
And hard worker it seemed to me,
And in those years
When the town was strong
He was definitely the man to see.

Farmers came
And brought their repairs
And they often asked his advice.
Then he got inspired
And right there in his shop
He invented a wonderful device.

A thrashing machine
With a brand new design
Was what it was when done.
It worked so well
That with patent in hand
He sold it for a considerable sum.

With all of his money
He moved out of state.
He could retire as he chose,
And no one came
To take over his job,
So the Iron Works had to close.

Now the building,
Its timbers rotting,
Is definitely falling apart.
Its doors are unhinged,
Its windows are shattered,
And just seeing it gave me a start.

I remember
How busy it was
In times of years gone by.
It seems to me
I can almost hear
Its ghosts who quietly cry.

THE APARTMENT BUILDING

On down some
Past the Iron Works block
Are the only apartments in town,
A big two-story
Rectangular thing
That seems to wear a frown.

Ugly then,
Still ugly now
And left with no one to care,
It was special
In my little boy's mind
For Bob and Norma lived there.

My Uncle Bob
With the crippled leg
Would always look after me,
And Aunt Norma,
His pretty young wife,
Was as nice as she could be.

After his wreck
Bob spent three years
Lying in a hospital bed.
So he taught himself
To play "Okie" guitar,
And became a musician instead.

When he got out
He started a band.
I liked to hear him play.
He loved the outdoors
And talked about fishing.
I remember all this to this day.

When I was a toddler
Norma worked at the store
And she too looked after me.
She helped me get dressed,
And she'd get me my breakfast,
And her smile was wonderful to see.

When they got married
They moved to the apartment
And I'd go and visit them there.
I liked being with them
And I liked spending time,
In the apartment at the top of the stair.

Despite the fact
That the building is ugly
And really has not been maintained,
I look at it fondly
And smile and recall
The memories that I have retained.

THE BANK

Right next door
To Grandma's store
Is the most curious thing of all –
A big old chunk
Of reinforced concrete
That stands about ten feet tall.

It's all that remains
Of the mercantile bank.
It's the vault with a big steel door.
A two-story building
Was built to go around it,
On purpose right next to the store.

When the town
Was really booming
And folks came to trade,
A nearby bank
Then did make it easy
For all transactions being made.

Then the stock market crash
Hit the economy hard,
And the bank went into decline.
Like so many others
It just never pulled out
So it closed its doors with a sign.

Instead of selling
Or changing their business
The owners walked off and left.
They left all the papers
And the furniture too
And people of their savings bereft.

So as kids
My friends and I
Used to joke and think it quite funny
To sneak in
Through a window
And use their checks for play money.

For a couple of years
There was a large family
That made their home upstairs.
They hung their laundry
Out both the side windows
And seemed to have serious cares.

Finally then
A health official came
And said their ills were their fault.
So the family left
And the bank was torn down,
And all that remains is the vault.

MY FRIEND'S HOUSE

Across from the bank
And down just one place
Was the home of my friend, Sandy.
It was painted all white
And had a shake shingle roof,
And a big open porch that was handy.

A number of children
Had been raised in that house,
And several had gone off to war.
Sandy, the youngest,
Was just about my age
And we played behind the store.

Our friend, Shirley,
Lived just up the hill,
And she always hung around.
We three played
With several other kids
And had the run of the town.

Then one day
Sandy's folks asked
If I could go to the lake.
His dad went to fish.
And Sandy'd go too
To take a swimming break.

My grandmother frowned,
And she thought for a bit,
Then said I really couldn't go.
I was unhappy
And couldn't understand
Her reason for just saying "no."

"It might not be safe,"
was all that she said.
Which was something I didn't like.
Instead she arranged
That I spend the whole day
At the farm of my best friend, Mike.

So I had a good time
Despite what was said,
And forgot as the day went along.
And when it got dark
Mike's dad brought me home.
To find there was sure something wrong.

There were cars on the street
And people stood around
Who seemed to be very morose.
My grandmother stopped
When she saw me come in,
And ran over and hugged me close.

With tears in her eyes
She said kind of softly
That Sandy and Shirley were dead,
And being so young
I didn't really understand
And asked her again what she said.

It was then that she told us
About a bad thing that happened,
And why she hugged me that way.
Then I understood
The decision she'd made
To keep me from going astray.

It apparently was
That after their picnic
Sandy's parents had gone off to fish.
Sandy and Shirley
And two older friends
Were left there to swim as they wished.

The one older boy
Found a makeshift wood raft
And thought they should go for a ride.
They got on together
And he pushed it way out
Then the straps it was bound with untied.

The raft came apart
And all four were dumped in
In water way over their heads.
The two older ones
Swam enough to find safety.
The two younger ones came up dead.

So Sandy and Shirley
Were drowned on that day,
But I lived to walk among men.
Now I look at the house
Where my friend and I played,
And I thank my grandmother again.

THE BROWN HOUSE

Across the street
From where Sandy lived,
And old brown house used to be.
It was run down
And used for a rental
And the property had nary a tree.

Behind the house
Was a big vacant lot
That was inviting on a nice summer day.
Sometimes I went
With my best friend, Mike
To make a kid's fort there and play.

There was a girl
That we'd seen at school
Whose family lived in that place.
She seemed nice,
But was just kind of quiet,
And watched us with a sad little face.

Once we went up
And started to talk
And asked her to help us, you see.
She said "Thanks."
But shook her head "No."
And seemed just as scared as could be.

I asked her why,
Because it was close
And her parents wouldn't think it a prank.
She shook her head strongly
And said that her mother
Said "no" and would probably spank.

Her mother had said
That their skin was brown.
They had come here to work just for now.
Our skin was white
And we lived in the town,
And that we were different somehow.

Her mom had said
That if our moms saw us,
Our folks would get really mad.
Then maybe our dads
Might come by to see them,
And do some things very bad.

Just then her mom
Called her into the house
And told us that we had to go.
We didn't understand then
What she meant by all that.
Consuela was her name, I know.

I asked my gram
What it was that they feared,
And would they be hurt in this place.
Her answer was straight.
Somewhere it might happen.
In our town it would be a disgrace.

THE METHODIST CHURCH

Just on up
That very same street
But over on the other side,
Sitting with aplomb,
White steeple intact,
Does the font of my religion abide.

My good grandma
Was an American Baptist
Who had no church around.
But she had to take
Her kids someplace nice
To know God's grace would abound.

So then she,
To be a good mom,
Went along with the Methodist way,
And then I,
When I came along,
Was raised the same in my day.

Sunday morning
After Saturday night bath,
I was all dressed up to the peak.
Polished shoes
And a part in my hair,
I was at my best for the week.

She took my hand
And we walked the block
And got there for Sunday School.
Then came church
And the singing of hymns
And Social Hour downstairs in the cool.

The feeling was good
And the people were nice
And a sense of community was high.
The stories I heard
About how to be good
Served well for all that I tried.

This time I went
Just to visit and see
What it felt like to walk in the door.
It still looks the same
And is still well maintained,
And the people are just like before.

Fewer people, for sure
And most I don't know,
But my memory fulfilled its desire,
And a picture hangs
On the wall in the back
Of my mom when she sang in the choir.

Just like it was
When I was so young
And needed that stability before,
Something came out
Of my trip to this place,
My roots found nourishment once more.

THE PUBLIC SCHOOL BUILDING

Just up the hill
From where the church is
Stands the biggest building in town.
It's the community school
That's been covered with stucco
That's so old it's turning gray-brown.

Now boarded up
With weeds in the yard
You can listen but hear nary a sound.
But I remember
When it thronged with young people
And was the happiest building around.

Children came running
At the sound of the bell
Brightly scrubbed and ready to learn.
Teachers were set
With good lesson plans
And diplomas for students to earn.

Gramma taught here
And my family attended,
And this is where I started school.
I didn't stay long,
But good things did happen
For I found book-learning a tool.

I had a good teacher
And I made some good friends.
I thought that learning was swell.
I even learned things
That weren't in text books,
And that can be important as well.

I learned to be quiet,
And I learned how to share,
And how to get along with the guys.
I learned about girls
And how to treat bullies,
And that planning my time would be wise.

I look at it now
And can't guess at the number
Of students that got their start here.
I do really wonder
If there might be a way
To save such a building so dear.

THE OIL COMPANY

Over kitty-corner
Across from the store
A small wood frame building resides.
Its two windows
Are all boarded up
And storage the only use it abides.

It once had a sign
That proclaimed "Oil Company"
In letters that were big and first rate.
It seems to have been
The first real gas station
Out in this part of the state.

It had two big pumps
With glass cylinder tops
That filled up with gas you could see.
Boxes of oil
In round quart containers
Were stacked everywhere they could be.

People would come
From all over the county
To gas up and then check their tires.
They'd have a chat
With the real friendly owner
And take care of their automotive desires.

Repair work was done
Back around on the side
Over by the big propane tanks.
Then come the winter
Tire chains were mounted
And radiators filled with much thanks.

Once in a while
When the temperature dropped
And your vehicle just wouldn't start,
You could certainly then
Call the owner to come over
And he'd jumpstart your car and depart.

Service today
Just doesn't match,
Even if the station is retail.
We didn't know
How lucky we were
When proprietors attended to detail.

THE "NEW" POST OFFICE

Across the street
Just north of the bank
A square cinder block building stands.
It was once built
To be the first Post Office
To meet the government's demands.

Built kind of small
But very efficient
It was good as government goes.
The trouble was
It had structural problems
And ultimately it had to close.

The postal clerk
Through most of its days
Was Myrtle, my grandma's best friend.
She was so nice
With a real gift of gab,
And everyone on her could depend.

Her husband, Grover,
Was really nice too.
For treats I had him to thank.
He'd been gassed
Back in World War I
And took oxygen from a tank.

I'd drop in at their home
About the middle of the morning
To sit around and have a little chat.
To my mock surprise
He'd then frequently offer
Some cookies she'd made just for that.

A cookie makes
A well meant gesture.
It's a special message it sends.
And both of them
Were awfully good
At being my special friends.

THE HIGHWAY STOP

On down from there
To the end of that street
The highway passed and all blessed.
There a restaurant stood
With gas station attached
That did pretty well more or less.

Farmers would come
For a fresh cup of coffee
Or maybe some ice cream to go.
Travelers would stop
To use the one restroom
And fill up with gas, don't you know.

A family owned it
And all helped to work.
It was definitely a family affair.
The dad ran the station,
And the mom was the cook.
All the kids helped out everywhere.

My buddy and I
Would walk to their store,
Or maybe we'd go with his dad.
I didn't notice
But then someone told me
That the younger girl liked me a tad.

What finally happened
To bankrupt this business
Has effected the town to this day.
The highway commission
Just to straighten out the road,
Moved the highway some two miles away.

UNCLE ART'S PLACE

Down the street
Back the other way
Almost down to the train station,
Stood another home
With a garden that testified
To the goodness of God's creation.

Uncle Art
Was Gramma's brother,
And Aunt Anna was her friend.
The salt of the earth
Was the term that applied.
Love directed their lives to the end.

Together they raised
On but minimum wages
One girl and four boys, all strong.
They managed to make it
Through Depression's tough times.
Not one of the kids came out wrong.

The boys all slept
Down in the basement
In one open big wide space.
Some boxing gloves
Were hung on the wall
To settle any in-house debates.

When they grew up
All the kids moved away
To seek their fortune and fame.
They did pretty well
Pursuing all their lives
For goodness was part of their game.

Dear Aunt Anna
Was very well known
Because of her exceptional garden.
She grew carrots and peas
And string beans and radishes,
But weeds she just couldn't pardon.

What I remember
When I went down to visit
Was finding her out by the cellar.
She showed me then
How to take a pea pod
And use my thumb as a sheller.

From that day on
I became a believer
In eating my vegetables raw.
It tasted so good
That it changed my ideas
And I tried every vegetable I saw.

After they died
Their old house was sold
And then it was finally torn down.
But I still remember
When I look at the lot
Just who had the best garden in town.

THE TRAIN STATION

The next block down
Has only one building.
It's where the train station stands.
After all this time
It's still well maintained
Because of the coal train's demands.

A small rectangle
Built to prescription
With attention to every detail,
It has one employee
To monitor the trains
And also take care of the mail.

I can remember
How it used to be done
To "post" the outgoing letters.
A big canvas bag
Was hung from a rod.
Then it was hooked off its fetters.

The railway employee
Was a dapper little man
With a well-trimmed brush mustache.
He tended to business
And got everything done
And he went everywhere on the dash.

His hairdresser wife
Was sweet and polite
And pleasant as she could be.
Sometimes my grandma
Would go down to see her
To have her hair permed, you see.

The train station was
Where Mom and I went
When it came time to go with my dad.
My eyes got all misty
And I cried a little bit.
Leaving home made me just really sad.

MIKE'S PLACE

Back up the street
Not far from the store
Stands a big old two-story place.
It sits dead square
Across two full lots
And straddles a wide open space.

It can't be missed
With its central location.
It's the biggest two-story you'll see.
You know that it's special
For another good reason,
It's been remodeled as nice as can be.

A long time ago
Mike's granddad had built it
For his family until he got old.
He raised up his kids
And lived out his life,
Then the home was eventually sold.

Owners and renters
Finally wore out the place
And moved leaving all the rooms bare.
With real estate waning
And the place all run down
It just sat there with no one to care.

Finally Mike bought it
And he then went to work
To restore it in the name of the family.
He replaced the roofing
And plumbing and wiring,
And he renewed things all quite amply.

Then there was sanding
And varnishing and painting –
All the fix-it jobs known to men.
When finally finished
It went without question
That is was back to its glory again.

He can be proud
Of his labor of love
And that this is something historic
It stands like a gem
In the middle of town,
And the feeling of pride is euphoric.

What it proclaims
To all who would look,
Is that someone has still really cared.
Just like I do,
He values this town,
And the memories that we both have shared.

EPILOGUE

Now I go back
To visit with Mike
And talk about memories amassed –
Some things forgotten,
But we can remind each other
So together we relive the past.

The fort in the weeds
Our friends there at school
And my days going out to his farm,
Uncle Bob flying kites,
And our riding our bikes,
It all comes back real and warm.

The various buildings
Bring back the memories
Of the people and events we knew.
The experiences we had,
Have stayed all inside us,
And helped us along as we grew.

One time we sat
On the store's front step
And drank a cold bottle of pop,
Then found the tattoo
That was stamped inside
When we pulled the cork from the top.

That tattoo imprint
From the pop bottle top
Was a short term image and clever.
The bigger imprinting
That we got from this town
Has shaped who we are - - forever.

"Oh little town of yesteryear.
How still I see thee yet,
But now I know
Because of you
My course in life was set.
The things I've had,
Both good and bad,
From you I can't forget."

Selected Poems

MY NEW HOME

On special assignment to
A Special Forces base camp
On the Cambodian border
For perimeter defense,

After twenty-five minutes
Of nothing but trees,
The mail chopper rolled in low
And made its approach.

Suddenly, there it was,
Carved out of the forest
A nine hundred yard bare spot
With a star in the middle.

The star- shaped configuration
Was four hundred yards
Of bulldozed dirt
With a barbed wire fringe.

Huddled in uneven groups
Inside it were a dozen or so
Tin roofed sand-bagged lumps
That passed for bunkers.

Criss-crossing between those
And the ammo box privies
Were connecting mud holes
That used to be roads.

In the center of the star
Like a big bull's-eye,
Sat the largest of the lumps
Festooned with antennas.

Placed around this lump
Were three reinforced parapets
From which came the snub noses
Of 105 mm. howitzers.

Spreading out from there
The entire area was sprinkled over
With ammo boxes and shell casings
Like a parmesan cheese topping.

All in all, Fire Base Katum
Had the appearance of
An infected ringworm blotch
On an unshaven face.

THE FAR EDGE OF DREAMS

We launch ourselves upon the path
    of glitter encrusted dreams
    in our youth and upward rising time
    and see, as visionaries see,
    a far horizon purple with the majesty
    of sunset as we imagine it will be.

We struggle and writhe and turn
    to free ourselves of the cocoon
    of our past and weaknesses
    and strive to emerge and spread our wings
    to begin our flight upward
    to where we think our spirit sings.

We take flight and set our course
    and rise to catch the breeze of fortune
    and, perchance, flutter a while
    and dance upon the air
    and view our world
    and think ourselves as blessed and faire.

But then we find the breeze is stiff
    and we loose our grip
    on the vision of our dreams
    and we are tumbled and thrown
    at the whim of forces
    of which we could not have earlier known.

We are bounced and punished
    and badly knocked around
    and we grasp at any handhold
    as we try to stop our rout
    and we want so ever badly
    to make it right and turn about.

But our strength has found its limits
    and we can only in part succeed
    as we try to find the course
    that we set for a goal once viewed
    and our vision is greatly clouded
    and our mind with mist imbued.

And as we fall as sunset
    far short of where we aimed
    with broken wings exhausted
    and flight no more becomes us
    the only mercy that we shall see
    is that Darkness which comes and numbs us.

A TRUTH

I went to a concert by
An amateur orchestra
New in our town
Just getting started.

The music was ambitious
But playing with spirit
And with a good soloist
They were doing well.

The piece was familiar,
A "war horse" of sorts
Full of great melodies
And moving rhythms.

I knew the piece well
And was enjoying it
As I looked around
At others in the hall.

I noticed one old man
Who looked European
With a balding spot
And small moustache.

He, nodding his head
Was swaying slightly
With all the rhythms
And watching closely.

After while he stopped
Just long enough
To pull out a tissue
And wipe his eyes.

It was plain to see
That he was crying
And continued so
Resuming his motion.

I was quite impressed
To see him so moved
By hearing the beauty
Of such great music.

I looked around again
To see who else might
Respond to the music
With the same heart.

There was one more
Who obviously felt
The same response
And the beauty there.

He was an old man
Of eighty years or so
He was slight of build
And he was Asian.

He nodded his head
Keeping perfect rhythm
Slightly more reserved
Than the other man.

He also seemed moved
Deep inside his heart
And shared like feelings
With the European man.

I then was moved by
The similarity of souls
Of two different people
Only so on the outside.

I was again convinced
Of the unity of people
And the universality
Of Music.

A SMILE

He was there,
Every time I came in,
Working behind the counter.

He cooked mostly,
And he spoke to the line workers
With gruff words in short sentences.

He was tall and slender,
In his forties and muscular,
With a craggy face and moustache.

He was Hispanic
As were the other workers
In this popular Mexican fast-serve.

But he was different,
In his silence and demeanor,
As if from living too hard a life.

Each time I came in
I seemed to catch his eye
As I placed my order for dinner.

It was unintentional,
And I kind of failed to react
For the first two times it happened.

Finally I realized
What kind of attitude
He must have thought he saw.

He didn't stare,
But his cold glance
Told me what was in his mind.

He didn't care for Gringos
Who thought they were above
The dark-skinned ones who served.

When this sank in,
I could not let it stand,
But countered with the only tool I had.

I smiled,
But not the perfunctory kind
That goes with saying "Thanks."

I looked deep into his eyes,
And smiled with my eyes,
And I nodded as if in salute.

It was his turn
To look astonished,
As I walked away with my food.

But the next time
I came in for dinner
And walked up to the counter,

He turned to look
And again our eyes met,
But now his smile came first.

It wasn't big,
But it was there,
On a proud face with softened eyes.

And I knew,
From that day on,
That we had bridged a gap.

Without a word exchanged,
We had given each other
The gift of respect and validity,

And we did it with a smile.

THE DINOSAUR'S CLUB

It all began one warm summer eve
When i was happily invited
To join a young people's party
Of our granddaughter's friends.

Conversing I spoke innocent words
That started with a pet phrase
That I've used many times before,
"I'll bet you dollars to donuts that–."

Someone looked at me and asked
"What does that saying mean–
What's with "dollars to donuts?
I've never heard that before."

I was really taken by surprise
And started out to try to explain
But realized it didn't really work
Since he didn't know about bets.

So someone else chimed in with
"It's OK, it's just a Pop-Popism,"
And that seemed to be enough
To help put the thing to rest.

That really piqued my curiosity
And I felt compelled to inquire
"What the heck is a Pop-Popism?
Would somebody fill me in here?

My granddaughter came to my aid
And said that all those quaint sayings
That I used each time I spoke
Her friends had never heard before.

She also said they had to assume
That I had made up all those things.
Since her name for me was Pop-Pop
Pop-Popisms became their name.

"Whoa now, Nellie" I had to say.
"You haven't understood me ever?"
"That's right" she said, "but it's OK.
We thought it was kind of cute."

So then I realized how big the gap
Between two generations and mine,
And the shock was really strong
To know I'd been patronized so long.

Being old means more than wrinkles
And if we don't "like pay attention,
We'll end up being as misunderstood
As was the other kind of dinosaur.

I SEEM TO DROP THINGS

I seem to drop things so easily now
As I go about my day.
For some reason I can't explain
My hands don't work too well.

I'm doing tasks I've done so long
By habit for many long years.
But all of a sudden things go awry
And a familiar item slips my grasp.

How'd that happen? I ask myself
As the item hits the floor.
And I can really see no cause
Why this should plague me so.

Then finally it dawns on me
That I'm older than I think,
And fingers don't work as well
Because they're dry and stiff.

Another reason comes to mind.
I've now lived so many years
That my brain is cluttered up
With way too many thoughts.

I'm no longer like that child
Who could concentrate so well.
Each task that he approached
Was his one and only aim.

So then I have to tell myself
That which I need to do.
When I attempt to do a job
I need to clear my mind.

I must pretend to be a child
And make each movement count
And focus on each step it takes
To control my world again.

EASING UP

I went out fishing today,
One of my favorite things
Through many a season
Since early in my youth.

I hadn't taken pole and creel
To find some water's edge
In well over a year or so
For ill health kept me down.

For all my life I had reveled
In fishing the wildest streams
And finding the remotest lakes
And conquering rough terrain.

With body strong and agile
And an attitude to match,
I'd leaped across wide chasms
And scaled tall canyon walls.

I'd waded swift flowing waters
And leapt from rock to rock
All with the fisherman's drive –
Cast my line to a better place.

I always pushed my body
And it served me very well
And no matter what I asked
It grew to meet my demands.

Through many years of fishing
My spirit thrilled and soared.
My joy was in more than sport
But in my love of all outdoors.

However, now in these last years
My body has begun to fail,
Parts of me that were so strong
Can no longer meet their tasks.

Old age is taking up my strength,
My lungs are shot as well.
My legs ache in an easy walk
And arthritis plagues my bones.

So as I lined my pole today
And tied on my trusty fly,
I looked at the path I'd taken
Way back in those early days.

Something told me "look again"
And I saw the challenges there.
But I saw a trail not quite as steep
That still offered up rewards.

I opted for the easier path
And made it through OK.
I caught some fish today –
Not like the days of yore.

But it was still a challenge
For this old body of mine
And tasting small successes
Can still give me my thrill.

So I recognized the wisdom
To choose the lesser path
And set my expectations
To heed my body's needs.

I could still find happiness
In the beauty that I saw.
It triggered many memories
Of all those years before.

HEALING

It was thirty-nine years ago
That fateful day
When I got a letter from our government
That started out "Greetings."

There was a war going on
Off in some southeast Asian country
That our leaders thought
Was in our best interests to fight.

Friends offered to make arrangements
To get me to Canada
So I wouldn't have to go
And have the experience of war.

But I had been raised
In the spirit of patriotism
And felt that I must do my part
As my father had.

So I went as I was ordered,
And was trained in the art of war,
With weapons and strategies
And the many ways of killing.

Then I was sent
Along with others like me
To a land of different-seeming people
With whom I had no quarrel.

I could not have known
What would happen there,
And my mind still boggles
At what I saw.

It is hard to imagine
What a bullet will do
Or the bodily damage
From a hand grenade.

Shrapnel in the right places
Can make you bleed like a sieve,
Or a claymore can take off your legs
And leave you still alive.

A nineteen year old kid
That I had trained myself
Took an RPG in the chest
And there was no flesh left there.

My best friend standing beside me
Was hit by an explosive round
And they took his extremities
Out separately from his body.

Those we called the enemy
Fared no better than we,
And the carnage we inflicted
Was just as bad or worse.

One cannot imagine
What napalm really does,
But when you see it
You know agony has no limit.

A beehive round fired point blank
From a 105 millimeter howitzer
Has the same effect of the body
As a huge meat grinder.

And those who were not the enemy
Who just happened to be in the way
Suffered no less and even more
Because they meant no harm.

And even if their bodies escaped
The rip and tear of steel,
Their homes and lives and livelihoods
Were shredded just as well.

All these things and more
Invade your consciousness,
And try as you might,
You cannot escape them.

They burrow inside you
While you're trying to stay alive,
And they hide in the recesses
Of your mind and soul.

Even though you return alive,
You don't leave them there,
And you carry them with you
As you try to get on with your life.

So I locked them up inside me
And pushed them out of sight,
And went on about my business
With a stiff upper lip.

A man must be strong
And control his real emotions
And be the kind of person
That others can count on.

So I lived my life
Trying to do good for others,
And provide home and sustenance
For a much loved family.

I didn't let those emotions show,
And I didn't talk about it much,
And only my wife knew
From some telltale signs.

For years, a car's backfire
Might drop me to the ground,
And if a war movie came on TV,
I was quick to change the channel.

After a number of years went by
I could talk about it a little
And even got to the point
That I could watch a combat show.

But all those memories
Were still wrapped up inside,
And they festered there
And my inner self had sickness.

I think I knew the trouble,
But had locked it in so long,
That there didn't seem to be a way
To purge it from myself.

Then late one night
I sat up alone
And spun the TV channels
To take away my restlessness.

And there was a movie,
With bloody combat scenes,
Not about my war
But about my father's.

I seemed compelled to watch,
And saw the same kinds of things
Presented there in make believe
That I had lived through myself.

And suddenly, without warning,
I began to cry,
And gentle tears flowing quietly
Turned into horrible aching spasms.

My being was wracked with pain,
And I tried to scream and couldn't,
And I convulsed with silent sobs
That put me on the floor.

Then slowly the agony lifted,
And I could open my eyes again,
And my muscles ached from tiredness,
But there was a different feeling there.

Somehow, all the horror
Had finally filtered out,
And the darkness in my soul
Seemed to have begun to clear.

Then the man I used to be
Before my time in Hell
Could recognize himself
As a living being still.

The knowledge finally hit me
Why this event had happened,
And despite my will's repression
Why these emotions had finally come.

It wasn't just my war
That had been so ghastly wrong,
But the compounding of all wars
Made the greatest of all man's sins.

And the moment of my realization
Drove all emotions to the top
And it blew away my fetters
And allowed my wound to drain.

My healing now may come
And I can be whole again,
And I have only but to hope
For mankind to heal as well.

All people need to realize
How wrong all wars have been
And force our leaders to come to terms
And heal our collective soul.

THE ROOM OF CRYSTAL CLEAR VISION

Somewhere behind your prefrontal lobe is an area yet unexplored, a room of crystal clear vision. You've never been there except on maybe one or two occasions when your eye caught a reflection from something beyond your normal ken. For a millisecond you knew in a way you'd never known before, and only the excitement of discovering precluded the serenity of knowing. Then it was gone and now you've forgotten it.

But the room is still there waiting, waiting for your liberation--the withdrawal of you from the time-space-emotion triangle—waiting for the unwrapping, the unveiling of your mind, your super consciousness, your Self. The time will come, oh silly man, when one by one you'll pull away the vestments, the wrappings, the bondage that you think is you but isn't. Off will come the image of your body, your strength, your wisdom, talent, fear, and predilection, and that thing which remains will rise slowly into the room. The clarity will blind you for a moment, but you'll adjust your vision and the intensity of awareness will become a need.

Awe and wonder will make you silent as you gaze down the tunnel you just traversed. There on the outside will be the world in which you lived, a million miles away. You'll watch the people and yourself like photo clips of old newsreels superimposed. You'll see the interactions, where they've been, where they are, and where they're going, all at once. Judgment will be yours with understanding, without malice, and without the distortion of the collage you once called yourself. Then all things in their disjunction and their continuity will have been resolved. They will trouble you no more.

You'll turn your gaze inward then to explore the length and breadth and contours of your new home. Each step inward will bring new reflections of light to absorb and know. Each knowing will be and existence complete and you'll pass from one to another by a compulsion gentle but inescapable. All of this will happen in the Now of that time. Each habitation of each existence will be as simultaneously enacted and space will be traversed by thought alone. Only intensity of being will vary in impending progression until you reach the end of the room.

A door lies at the end of this room, a door you will eventually face. Then the decision will be yours, to go through and gain what? You won't know. Perhaps it will be total freedom and a oneness with the universe. Perhaps it will be, and you will be—nothingness. Or you can go back the way you came to where you were. You won't be as you were, but then who would? The decision would be yours.

All this will come, oh silly man, in eons yet to pass, when you reach the room of crystal clear

Vision.

CLOSE TIES

One early morning
When my wife and I
Went out for breakfast
For a good start to the week.

We were walking
Toward the front door
Of a favorite restaurant
In our local neighborhood.

Two other people
Got to the door first
And made their way in
As we stood and watched.

Both were disabled
With one being blind
With a red tipped stick
And the other with a walker.

We looked closely
And decided for sure
They were likely brothers
From their facial features and all.

The older crippled one
Gave the other instructions
To find and hold open the door
So they could both go inside to eat.

They navigated it well
And worked as a team
To get where they needed
With some ease and satisfaction.

We watched as they sat
And the one took the menu
And gave the other his choices
That made the younger one smile.

The older one watched
Giving directions to utensils
And other items on the table
So the other could find his way.

The younger sibling
Seemed to make a map
Of the table top topography
Forming a picture in his mind.

Then they both ate
Enjoying their repast
Having good conversation
And sharing in the day's events.

When they finished
The younger man rose
Feeling his way around
To where the older man sat.

He put out a hand
That the older man took
And together they got him
Up and positioned on his walker.

They then as a team
Walked to the check-out
Where the older paid the bill
And they walked out the door.

I watched them go
Across the parking lot
Arm in arm in closeness
With each helping the other.

It occurred to me
That our whole world
Is likewise incapacitated –
We could learn something here.

BITTERSWEET

I sat across from them
With my wife of many years
In the next row of tables
In a fashionable fast-food restaurant.

They were older than we
By fifteen to twenty years,
And from what I could see
Were showing the results of age.

She was in her seventies,
With a pinched face,
Blanched-out complexion,
And age spots on her arms.

She wore a silk blouse,
Fitted skirt with a belt,
And a bouffant hair-do
That came from a shop.

Her eyes were narrowed
And she wore a frown
As she spoke to him
In a somewhat terse manner.

He seemed to be a little older,
In his early eighties,
And he had aged badly
In both body and mind.

His muscles had shriveled
And he seemed kind of gaunt,
And you could see the tendons
Stick out around his neck.

He didn't say much
As he continued to eat,
And he looked at her
With a kind of blank look.

He almost seemed
To not be focused
On what she was saying
Despite her pointed remarks.

Perhaps his mind
Had begun to slip
From advanced age
Or maybe verbal assault.

She was lecturing him
On what he should do
Or possibly shouldn't do
In tones that showed frustration.

Finally the waiter
Left the receipt for the bill
That she had paid
With her credit card.

She put her card
In her purse
And stood up to leave,
And he just sat there staring.

She turned to him
And in acid tones
Said "Come along, Harry,
We have to leave."

He finally swiped at his mouth
With the napkin from his lap,
And pulled himself up
From the curved booth seat.

She took his arm
And maneuvered him out,
Around the tables
And toward the door.

But the look on her face
Told a double-edged story
For her jaw was clenched
But her eyes showed a smile.

And I realized as I looked
Her own need to take care,
For her frustration only masked
Her greater need for dominance.

OUT FOR A SPIN

Chug, chug, chug
the pistons of life go churning
in cars beside the road
and other places.
The bushes hide the motion
of internal combustion
on an evening spin
when the motor's warm.
And the power is there
with the throb of acceleration
down the road
running without brakes.
The rhythm of the shaft
opens and closes valves
to knock the carbon off the soul
'til exhaustion.
And when its over
the human gears have gone partway
toward wracking up their mileage
of being.

TOUCHING

I went to see her, this woman of my blood.
She was little and shriveled up, in a wheel chair.
The nursing home looked nice but smelled of urine,
So an attendant wheeled her out to the sun deck.

She was dressed in a new red running suit
And had a pretty red bow in her thinning hair.
All her life she had refused to wear red clothing,
But here she was, dressed up fit to kill.

She was smiling at us as best she could.
She was a little self conscious about that
Because one of the other residents
Had slipped in and stolen her teeth.

She greeted us and called us by name.
We were surprised, my wife and I,
Because my uncle, her son, was sure
That she wouldn't recognize us now.

She wanted to know how our lives were going,
Us and our kids and our grandkids.
She was happy to hear about each as we told,
Although she got the names mixed up a bit.

We were glad to see her memory still there,
As she brought up old stories and times,
And were amazed at some tears that came,
Because she'd been our pillar of strength.

Her own life had been as hard as it comes,
As a widow with two kids in the Depression.
But each of us grandkids had been taken in
To her home and her heart as we needed.

We were nurtured, and guided, and taught
In her strong minded yet gentle ways,
And we owed her for much that we knew,
And not the least for our own strength too.

I tried to tell her in true simple words
How much she had meant in my life,
And what a void for me she had filled.
Then she smiled a bit and fell silent.

She hadn't been one for display of emotion
And touching for closeness was improper,
But for some reason now I reached out to her,
And put my hand lightly on her cheek.

She reached up and grasped my hand hard
And pushed it against the side of her face.
She leaned into my outstretched fingers
With as much strength as her poor body had.

Her eyes went closed and her face contorted
As she strained to feel my touch on her face.
And I could do nothing but sit there amazed
As she assuaged a great yearning need.

I realized as I watched and caressed her face,
That I was learning again at her side.
This lesson in life would apply to me too,
And my knowing would in some way help.

As each of us nears the end of our life,
And we are about to depart this plane,
Then the simple act of a physical touch
Will remind us of where we've been.

Regardless of where we go when we die,
We cherish our life in its physical form
And the touch and caress of a loved one
Is a remembrance of our presence here.

(To my Gramma Peg)

TO ROBERT S. ON VETERAN'S DAY

Hey, Bob, aren't you a little young for this.
I mean, hell, you just barely turned nineteen.
And jeez, you've even still got adolescent zits.
You ain't even really had a real girlfriend yet.
Yea, I know that the jobs were scarce at home
And the recruiter seemed like a really nice guy.
I know, my dad defended the good old U.S. too,
And coming here was the patriotic thing to do.
But shit, man, this is really not the way to go.
I mean, what in heck are we doing here really?
We're supposed to be fighting Communism
And defending our country and all that stuff.
But this place doesn't look like our country.
It isn't ours and never was and never will be.
It really belongs to the guys we're fighting.
It's their country and it's their government,
Why don't we leave it to them to work out?
Then we wouldn't have had to go through this,
I mean, basic training and our leaving home,
And learning how to shoot and kill and stuff.
Hell, man, I remember the day you came in.
You grinned at me and said "Put me to work."
So I trained you and wised you up a little.
You learned fast, man, and did a good job.

I told you not to take your shirt off outside,
"Cause your blond hair and super white skin
Made you a target for snipers and all that.
I taught you how to work the firing charts
And how to talk to the F.O.s out in the field.
You already knew the gun directions lingo
Because you'd volunteered to try the FDC
And came in off the guns to help us out.
We became buddies and talking was easy.
We got to know each other pretty well.
We went through the hairy times together
Between the mortar fire and the RPGs
And this last ground attack was the shits.
We took some really bad stuff this time,
But you and I stuck together all the way.
I guess that's why I'm doing this job now,
Cleaning your guts and flesh off the radios,
And waiting for the medics with a body bag.

Hey, just remembering our time together.
Anyway – Happy Veterans Day

FOR A FRIEND

I do not cry at funerals.
You see, a man must be strong
as I had to be at twenty-one
when my mother killed herself,
and I had to be there for my brother.

I could not cry for I was drained
Of emotion and almost of hope in Viet Nam
As I watched my comrades, young boys mostly,
Get cut down or blown apart around me
And I steeled myself to stay alive.

Nor could I cry as my gut was clamped
In an aching silent scream
When the doctor came out of the operating room
And said our child had not developed right and died
And there was no funeral.

And as I gripped my own father's hand
When he convulsed in the agony of chemotherapy
And then died with the look of fear on his face,
I could not cry but rather raged in frustration
at a hospital that overdosed him.

Today, at the funeral of a friend, I cried,
a little because he was a man of God cut down,
a little because his family had to give him up,
a little because he was a good man gone,
but mostly because I had lost a friend.

You see, today, as I face my waning years,
And I let down my guard in the quietness of age
I am left with one real and reassuring truth,
That to be able to cry for the loss of a friend
Affirms the value of that friendship—

And that affirms the value of having lived at all.

IN MY WAR

I read an article today
in the newspaper
that said that people should take their children
to see a certain movie about war.

The movie was made
by someone famous for graphic depiction
and visual images bigger than life.
The movie was a three hour blood bath.

The article said children should see it
so they would know about war
and how awful it is.
Perhaps this is so.

Hopefully, this is the closest they'll get.
Hopefully they won't get as close as I did.
Because it was a little different,
in my war.

When you sit in the theater
and you see someone get hit in the chest
with an explosive round
you don't have to wipe the flesh off your face.

Or when a grenade lands in your bunker
and blows off your best friend's legs
and you're screaming into the radio
for air support.

you don't have to feel him tugging
at your arm in shock asking
"I'm going to be all right, aren't I?
I'm going to be all right, aren't I?"

Or when your position is under assault
and your spotter outside yells into the phone
"They're coming through the barbed wire!"
just before his line goes dead.

then you lie down on the floor,
point your rifle at the door of the bunker,
and pray that you'll still be alive
five minutes from now.

That's a little different from wondering
if there's going to be an intermission
so you can go out and buy popcorn,
or a big orange drink.

In the movie an officer comes up with
an ingenious method of disabling tanks.
In my war an officer ordered us to rebuild our bunker
even though we told him the walls would be too thin.

The night after we finished the rebuild
we came under attack.
We lost one dead and three wounded
when a rocket-powered grenade came through the walls.

A movie sergeant heroically disabled an enemy machine gun.
One of our sergeants broke a toe diving for his bunker
instead of manning his gun or directing his men.
He got a Purple Heart and a Bronze Star anyway.

In the movie a battalion commander dies leading his troops
In an airdrop behind enemy lines.
Our unit commander stayed behind in the rear area
and flew by helicopter to our position once a month.

If it was quiet he'd land,
do a ten minute inspection and leave.
If there was any enemy fire in the area,
he'd turn back without ever getting "in range."

In the movie, the local civilians
wanted to be "liberated."
In my war we had two hundred and fifty local militia
helping to defend our position.

WE had to go around the perimeter
twice a week with wire cutters
to cut the communication lines locals had run
to give the enemy strategic inside information.

In the movie the allied invasion
was a brilliant work of strategy
that changed the tide of battle
and finally won the war.

In my war our intelligences sources
brought us information on a regular basis
that would have brought us victory after victory,
but our superiors had their orders.

"String it out a little longer.
We have more guns to sell.
We'll all line our pockets.
and the troops can go to hell."

And when I got back Stateside
and was nursing the wounds in my body and soul,
I listened to the reports
of civil unrest, demonstration, and hatred.

Those of us who had obeyed our country's call
and followed in our father's patriotic steps,
we who had given up our lives, careers
and body parts,

were despised as killers, shills
and warmongers,
who dared not wear our uniforms
among those people we thought we were defending.

Yes, take your child to see the movie.
Buy them some popcorn,
and comfort them in the middle of the night,
when they wake up dreaming of death and dismemberment.

Hopefully, that's as close as they will get,
and that's as much as they will need to learn.
Hopefully they won't get as close as I did
in my war.

LESSON LEARNED

I helped a child today
Who came to me dejected.
She's in love with the violin
But doesn't know how to play.

It seems she'd got a start
But hadn't learned the way
That would put her on the road
To playing as an art.

And being the type of kid
Who cares a very lot,
She'd tried her very best
To learn what she was taught.

I could tell just from her sound
That she'd tied herself in knots
And tightened up her muscles
So each tune gave her a tussle.

She couldn't play but a little bit
And was dejected to the point
Of asking through her tears
If I felt that she should quit.

But I remember something
That told me what to say.
Because I had needed help
Way back along my way.

I'd gotten a bad beginning
To my academic life
For no one had ever taught me
The basic things, you see.

I didn't know my alphabet
And counting was barely set.
I didn't know the process
To add or subtract as yet.

All the other students
In my homeroom it's true
Had done all this before.
But I really had no clue.

I made some awful errors
And the other students laughed.
Not knowing how to handle it,
I pretended to be daft.

So I became the class's clown
And entertained them some,
And went on for several years
Just thinking I was dumb.

Until finally at a higher grade
A teacher saw my plight
And started out to salvage me
And help me see the light.

She had the care and patience
To decide what I had missed,
And then figured the best way
To come to my assist.

She built upon what little I knew
And added new skills each day.
She also changed my attitude
And gave hope along the way.

The outcome of her efforts was
That I caught up with my class
And even developed skills
To do much more than pass.

So as I looked at this girl today
My heart went out to her,
And I knew I could find a way
To help her learn to play.

YEARS HENCE

When I was young
And had on occasion
To deal with older people,
I did not understand them.

I could not visualize
Their trials and tribulations
Or how their bodies felt
Or why they moved so slow,

Or why they grimaced
In climbing a stair,
Or why they were afraid
Of fainting and falling down,

Or why it took both hands
To put a key in a door,
Or how they could forget
What they came in for.

To me an old person
Was a different creature
With feelings I couldn't share.
But years hence, now I can.

TRILOGY

One Choice

The sunrise meets an early death at dusk
And wonders why the vacancy of days has been.
There is no shelter now in aging
in the bower of dreams spun out
and the sunlight of "Paradise" radiates an end
to a parched and addled brain.

The days were hollow and reeked of chloroform,
Senility was at the beginning, not the end,
and vacuous prattle of emotions made a cloud
over our eyes to talk about but not to feel.

We reached to the stars but were standing upside down,
and grasped our roots and pulled, and our fathers died,
and we went floating free in a nothingness of our own making,
and we missed more than we knew.

Our comet died before it reached the heavens,
and simply disintegrated in a weak shower of sparks.
Our only hope would be that a spark or two
may hit on tindered ground
so that although we shine no more
a portion of our fire may live
and raise a brightness yet to glimmer
on the shelf of Heaven.

The Alternative

Ah, but rather we might stand
where time stands still,
and look upon our "now" as "always."
So instead of looking out – look in,
and seek our soul on the Edge of Forever.

For when we look, what we see
is not our bones or heaps of clay,
but a fire kindled before our keening
that is burnt deep in the sands of time
and runs through us on its way to all life's destination.
And it's not a flicker, but a glow like red hot coals,
whose warmth is stronger and goes deeper into the
void of nothingness that your eyes can see.

Then we realize the reason for our consciousness
was to feel this warmth,
and the reason for living
was to feed this flame
by every movement of our coming and going,
and by adding to it day by day
we build on our testament in Heaven.
And all we have to do is look,
and at that looking we may
go inside every moment of our allotted time
to stretch it towards infinity.
With that, Time stands still,
and we fear no more Death.

The Outcome

Hence we dream our dreams, and run our course,
and strike a path for others.
Then we make our leap to the Chariot of the Sun
and share a handshake with our Fathers.

We stand a moment on the edge of Now
and then go about our ways,
and warm ourselves from time to time
by sneaking a peek at the fire.
For what we see is for all mankind
and it looks like a mighty river,
and it feeds from what we do while we're here
for the good of one another.

So, before our days have reached their end,
and our comet has streaked the sky,
we must try to add to the river's flow
with each moment that goes by.

By giving love at each moment's turn
to those we stand beside,
we birth a shower of sparks that fall
and merge with that lighted way.
This brands our path to Heaven's Gate
and leads us to Eternal Day.

GOLFING BUDDIES

I watched these two old men
Sitting at their table
Holding up a golf scorecard
And talking animatedly.

They had obviously been
To a local golf course
And had just played
Their morning round.

Their hair was grey,
Their arms were tanned,
And their faces showed
The lines of age.

They wore flowered shirts
And on their chairs
Were Arnold Palmer style sweaters
The kind you can't buy any more.

One seemed to be a bit older
Than the other
But they were obviously
Friends of long standing.

It made me think
Of my own father
And how we used to try
To play golf together.

We were friends
But we had some problems –
I was young and egotistic,
And I didn't like his "coaching."

He was so studied
And read all the How-To books
And took forever, I thought
To line up his shots.

The outcome was
That I found excuses
To have to work
When he wanted to play

He was disappointed
But tried to understand
As I wandered away
From the one thing we shared.

Then he got sick
And couldn't play at all
And he suffered a while
And then passed away.

Now I watch those two old men
Who have something to share,
And know that Dad and I
Should have "stayed the course."

PROGRESSION

When we were quite young
The death of someone known,
An older relative, perhaps,
Was simply a family event
That was attended to dutifully,
Then we went about our lives.

Then becoming young adults
The death of a grandparent
Or accidental death of a friend
Struck us quite emotionally,
And moved us to heavy tears,
And we knew not how or why.

As we grew to our maturity
With young families of our own,
And we watched our parents die,
We sensed the progression of days,
And then valuing life even more
We strove to protect our own.

Now, as we enter our final phase
We feel the chill of dead cold bones,
And we savor the warmth of life,
So we dote on the morning sunrise
And revel in the beauty of children,
And we wait to be no more.

ROCKWELL MATERIAL

It was a "family" restaurant,
Not the old-fashioned corner diner
Made famous by Norman Rockwell,
But a modern national chain variety.

I walked through the door
Into the air-conditioned ante-way,
Glad to get into the cool and comfort
Of escaping the late summer evening heat.

I glanced through the window
At the seating area closest to the counter
Where the booths are just big enough for two,
And there they were, right there in front of me.

The two sat in the booth
Across from each other but coupled
In the framing of an Evening Post cover
By the window that kept me outside their sphere.

They were both past seventy,
But they were obviously out on a date,
And though the man was the only one that spoke,
The interaction of chemistry was something to watch.

He was dressed casual,
And he really needed a haircut
Because shocks of hair stood out
As he rubbed his head when he spoke.

He spoke animatedly
As he leaned forward on his elbow,
And he talked like he really needed to talk,
And it was obvious that the conversation was all his.

She, on the other had,
Sat upright on the bench seat,
With her hands folded in her lap,
And her attention was focused all on him.

She wore a pretty pink dress
That had little bouffant sleeves
With a full skirt that covered her knees
And the whole thing shimmered with sparkles.

Her hair was put up
In a neat fifties era style,
And her makeup was tasteful
As it tried to add color and hid wrinkles.

She sat perfectly still,
And tried not to interrupt
As he held forth at great length
Explaining what was wrong with the world.

But the look on her face
,Told me just what she felt
As she smiled her sweet smile
And listened an looked happily at him.

It was nice to have someone
Who'd take her out on the town
And who was at ease enough with her
To share his thoughts, feelings and opinions

It was enough to know
That someone needed her there
As she basked in much needed attention
And could feel important in real human terms.

In each other's presence
They found something to share,
And that's what I saw as I stood there
And was allowed into this little tableau.

The window frame picture
Had told a truth without words,
And then I, like Norman Rockwell,
Witnessed an unfolding human story.

FOR BARBARA RICHARDS

Gentle spirits do not wait upon the hour,
but come and go as time flits by.
And we shall have them as they choose
and love them as we can.

We cannot hope to hold them long
or tie them to this earthly vale.
We clutch them close and see their beauty,
and then they fly to more fitting worlds.

Our souls respond to this shared embrace,
and grow in depth and clarity.
We then can go upon our way
and try to make our reflection theirs.

MEMORIES

Sitting in a doctor's office
Waiting room

Of a respected doctor who
Specializes

In old people's problems
Or geriatrics,

I, myself, had finally com
Face-to-face

With some problems with
My plumbing.

As I sat thumbing through
A magazine

And waiting impatiently for
My turn,

A much older gentleman
Came in

And took a seat right next
To mine.

Shortly after he got himself
Comfortable,

A young woman came into
The room.

He watched as she walked to
A chair.

She was as young as maybe
Thirty-two,

She was pert and still had a
Girlish figure.

I watched him watch her as
She sat.

His gaze was intent as she crossed
Her legs,

Soon I saw a little smile start
To show,

And his eyes took on a twinkle
Of knowing look.

Then his gaze seemed to refocus
Far away,

As the smile on his face seemed
To soften.

And I suspected that I knew
His thoughts.

That better days were gone but
Not forgotten.

GETTING ON (OVER THE HILL)

Growing old, it's said
Has its ups and downs,
And some of it
Ain't fun and clowns.

It's for a fact
That our bodies ache,
And problems come
That keep us awake.

We're like a car
That once was new
And problems come
That turn us blue.

Our bushings erode
And seals do leak.
Our transmission has
An ornery streak.

Our battery's weak,
Our valves don't close.
Our fuel line's plugged
And we've a leaky hose.

Our upholstery's worn,
Our windshield's fogged,
Our horsepower's down,
Our carburetor's clogged.

And what do we know
About fixin' all this?
There is no promise
Of healthful bliss.

And doctor's fees
And hospital care
Run up some bills
That make us stare.

So all we can do
With power of will
Is shuffle along   On over the hill.

MR. GUITAR MAN

We walked into the dining area
Of one of our favorite restaurants
On a late night Rest and Recoup
After a hard evening's work.

Our hostess wound us through
Past several occupied tables
To have us take our seats
At a booth on the far wall.

We settled down with menus
To figure out what we wanted,
To order from our waitress,
And to have a look around.

The sudden twang of a guitar
Brought my head up quickly,
And there, two tables away,
Was a strange sight indeed.

Sitting over there in a booth
On the wall ten feet away
Was a rumpled looking man
In blue-jean pants and jacket.

With hair long and uncombed
And beard at least a week old,
He seemed to be about sixty
And probably down on his luck.

Before him out on the table
Lying there without any case,
Face up in shiny resplendence
Was a gorgeous electric guitar.

It was blue with the six strings
And gold knobs and vib lever
Designed for a lead guitarist
From some 60s era rock group.

He was just sitting there
His cup of coffee to the side,
Staring at this shiny guitar,
Sometimes plucking a string.

Occasionally people passed
And stopped to ask a question,
Reaching to also pluck a string,
Then smiling would pass on by.

I could hear bits of conversation
Like "Gee, mister, what kind is it?"
And, "a Fender custom design,"
And "Yea, it was made for me."

Every once in a while I'd hear
"Well, whatcha doin' with it?"
Then he'd mumble something,
But finally, "I guess it's for sale."

Between visits and coffee refills
He would simply sit and stare
Or wipe off a smudge he saw
And occasionally pluck a string.

Finally, someone walked up
Who picked up the blue beauty,
Felt its heft, and asked a price,
To which the man looked startled.

He hesitated, he thought a bit,
And then sadly said his price,
To which the other responded
By nodding to clinch the sale.

The money was handed over
The buyer, smiling, walked off,
And then the old man was left alone,
To sit and collect his thoughts.

He looked out the window a bit,
Then turning he took his napkin
And wiped away some tears,
Then quietly got up and left.

TO MELISSA

How should we
As musicians be
When all is said and done?

When we have reached
The end of our road
And come to our double bar,

Will we regret
What we have set
When we have gone that far.

For as we go
From day to day
Playing notes we have to play,

We have choices
That come along
That blend together as our song.

So what we choose
Is what we are
As we follow our own star,

And what we make
Is what we take
When we leave life's concert hall.

So don't lose sight
Of your first goals
When you're up against the wall,

And try each time
You stop and look
To be true to you inner book,

For in that book
Your heart wrote true
What it knows for sure is you.

We all start out
To pursue an art
That is the expression of our soul.

We play for love
And love to play
To pursue a higher self,

And it would be
A crime, you see
To lose that along the way.

Love,
Pop-Pop
Christmas 2004

COFFEE TIME

12:30 a.m.
We sit drinking coffee,
Coffee from the wash boy's well.
We talk about home.

The radios are quiet.
He's come in from his gun.
He's homesick at nineteen.
We talk behind ammo box walls.

The night isn't so bad
When we can talk like this,
Laugh at the rats
And the mail plane that didn't bring mail.

He stands up to pour some more coffee
And there it is---Whump!
The intercom crackles with "Incoming!"
Then Whump! Whump! Whump!

He stops in his stride
As I dive for the phone saying
"Christ, it's coming in fast!"
Then it happens.

Wham! I go down
And the lights go out,
Then I'm up again
Screaming at the guns for fire.

The intercom's yelling
"They're on the north wire!"
I put number three to the north,
And I'm wet down my back, and sticky.

The tracers go by
Past a hole in the wall.
Number two gun isn't there any more,
And I kick something soft in the dark.

"Give me fire on the north!"
"Get a gunship up here!
Then a voice on the floor says
"I don't hurt, I'm OK, aren't I?"

Number one gun's shooting over the roof.
"Watch the God damn antennas!" I yell.
The voice on the floor has a leg in four angles.
"Yea, you're all right. Take it easy."

The call comes in, "This is Spooky Number One".
"Give me fire all around!" I say.
The gun ship opens up,
But the voice on the floor isn't talking.

Thirty minutes later,
When the fight's died down,
Medivac comes in
And they take him away.

So now I'll go on
To patch up the wall,
Wash his blood off my back,
And get some more water for coffee.

OLD SOLDIERS

We are a strange lot,
We old military men,
Those of us who survive
To live our lives after combat.

In our first few years back home
We really have some trouble
Losing the survival responses,
That kept us alive in our wars.

My wife got kind of used to me
As I'd hit the dirt instinctively
When passing cars would backfire
And I wanted to yell "Incoming!"

Some responses faded with time,
But some were more insidious,
Like my being a lot more quiet
And perhaps a bit more distant.

My driving a car changed also.
Having seen death first hand
I learned to value life intensely.
And became a lot more careful.

When scanning television channels
If a war movie came up on the screen
I was really fast changing channels.
I wouldn't look at what I'd seen before.

Dreams at night were even worse.
I ran through jungles escaping capture
And engaged in firefights with my M-16.
It never changed as years went by.

Finally I had to face my foe
And find the demon in my soul.
I forced myself to look at wars
And see the folly of them all.

In a fit of sobbing, crying, gasping
I purged the darkness torturing me
And finally stood straight and tall
And talked again with ease and life.

Wars since mine have come and gone
And all produced the same effect.
As soldiers returned to face their lives
I knew they would be hurt inside.

I saw the evidence of this today
In my old age and infirmity
As I lay there in a hospital bed
And waited to see my doctor.

An old man in the bed beside me
Was listening to someone next door.
It was the voice of another old man
Who was crying and shouting orders.

My roomy said "I know those orders.
The man in there was an officer.
I think he was in the artillery.
He must have lost that battle."

I thought to myself without saying
"Yes, he lost that battle years ago
and returns to fight it now again.
I know he will lose this one also."

GOOD MEDICINE

Those who have lived
For a very long time
Have seen as much
As anyone should.

Time is a juggernaut
That does have a way
Of rolling most heavily
Across everyone's life.

And it is most disturbing
And usually destructive
And it does take its toll
No matter who you see.

The lines on the faces
Belie the physical strain
And the look in the eyes
Show the emotional pain.

Events one lives through
Are often unwished for
And some we do wish for
Very often go wrong.

A lifetime of this dealing
With events so contrary
Does color one's vision.
And rests hard on the soul.

How one then holds up
Is a measure of their will
For fighting off negatives
Takes unusual strength.

Not everyone manages
To hold up as they go
To find one is special
You should take note.

When someone lives
A long and hard life
And they can still laugh
Taking all in their stride,

We know we have met
An exceptional person
So we can gain strength
From this happy thing,

For it raises our spirits
And shows us the way
To model our own lives
Seeing old people smile.

MY KIND OF RESAURANT

I sit, pensively, sunk in somewhat
    in the overstuffed seat of a booth by the window.
My forearms rest gratefully on the table top
    that is cool from being under the AC vent.

The recorded sound of a country-western singer penetrates
    through the gaggle of voices that pervade the room.
The jammed guitar chords penetrate my auditory consciousness
    Like short jabs with a blunt stick.

A cup of tea sits steeping in front of me
    with steam rising from the brown liquid surface.
The waitress couldn't find a lid for the teapot,
    so she nestled a condiment cup in the hole.

I look across the room to see the mostly-white heads
    of elderly and somewhat addled Midwesterners.
They come here to get the bland foods they grew up with,
    and that now won't irritate their stomachs.

I listen and their conversations are about little things
    that in their own minds have grown big.
This is perhaps because their memories have dimmed
    and therefore they can't remember their bigger cares.

I notice for a moment my own white head
    in the reflection of the window.
Somehow it seems strange to me
    that the person that I see there is me.

Then I turn my attention to another bite
    of my nice grilled cheese sandwich.
I wonder if they buttered the bread
    on the inside before they grilled it.

RUMINATING

In lives embroiled in wondering
Where is it we shall go?

We try to see what the future holds
But with heads as white as snow.

Our meager means of self support
Shrinks with our remaining years.

Our bodies falter in various parts
And pain promotes our tears.

Things we thought were little once
Stand firmly in our way.

And we live in fear of accident
As our bones go towards decay.

We try to avoid introductions all
For fear of forgetting a name,

We're also afraid to leave the house
Without our trusty cane.

Our friends are steadily dying off
And we feel still more alone,

And sometimes spend an hour or so
Just waiting by the phone.

Our family members move away
Or perhaps avoid our door

Because they live at a faster pace
And it hurts us to our core.

The soul's survival concerns us now
If our maker we shall see,

But afraid, as much as anything,
That we'll just cease to be.

We wonder for our families
If we've done the best we can,

And did we really contribute much
To the good of our fellow man.

And while we sit awondering,
Fate brings us to an end,

And wondering was all for naught,
On that you can depend.

AN OLD HOME IN NEBRASKA

What work of wood and stone
I see here
Amazes me.

The skill and craft of construction
Far surpasses
Houses of today.

This is exceptional because the lumber
Was rough cut
By an early mill.

The carpenter was also the stonemason
And the work of both
Took intelligence and pride.

It has been many years since it was abandoned
But the walls still stand
And the roof is intact.

Two outbuildings housed a blacksmith shop and a stable
With a corral
And a feed lot.

It was the microcosm of a self-sufficient world
That supported life
And withstood time.

There was a man-made pond out back
To raise fish
And for children to play by.

A whole arbor of trees was planted
For their fruit
And for shade.

A large family was raised here
There were five boys
And five girls.

All ten came up strong and survived
Save one girl
Who died of illness.

That one was buried lovingly under a tree
Planted by her father
And watered by her mother's tears.

Cattle raising and cow ponies was the family business
And all helped
Whatever way needed.

A small one room school provided education
And all kids attended
At least through sixth grade.

School was interrupted only for work
For all helped with roundup
And planting and harvest.

Sometimes after a week's effort
Saturday night gave rise
To family-made music.

The homebuilder and good father of all
Played an accordion
Brought from Denmark.

One child played a fiddle cut from cottonwood
Another a cheap harmonica
And the rest all sang.

It was a good, strong, loving, and a wonderful life
Where all children thrived
And adults were fulfilled.

Then times changed, children grew up and left
When the dust bowl came
And the economy crashed.

As it happens with the passage of time,
The good mother died
So the father moved away.

I view it all now these many years later
With imagination
And with some tears.

A myriad of things passes through my mind
And my inner ear responds
And I hear things.

These are the sounds of twelve people's lives,
Sounds of saws and hammers
And hooves in a corral.

I hear much of gladness and some sadness
With both children's laughter
And a mother's crying.

I hear children in a little boat on a pond
And a cottonwood fiddle tune
And an old accordion.

These sounds came to touch my soul-
They are of my family
And in my heart.

A NEW WRINKLE

Sometimes I don't see too well
Right after I get up
And sometimes it's hard
To actually look in the mirror.

Today I had to get ready to go
Out with some friends
And I needed to try hard
To get my old eyes to focus.

So after squinting a few times
I cleared the haze
And stared into the mirror
To see what my face was like.

Well now that was a surprise.
It gave me a start
To come face to face
With a much wrinkled old man.

"Gee, is that me?" I stammered.
That face looks like
The worst patch of erosion
In Hell after a major rain storm.

"Where did I get all those wrinkles?
What a mug!"
Life must have been bad
To bring out all those creases.

Let me see if I can figure it out.
Some bad times?
Life hasn't been easy.
It's kicked me around a bit.

Loosing Mom when I was young,
Having to look after
My little brother then
And help him understand "Why?"

Then there was getting drafted,
Being sent to war,
And seeing people die,
And almost being killed myself.

Then after I married my wife,
And she got pregnant,
Something went wrong.
We lost our chance for children.

And after working hard at my job
And saving money
And getting enough to invest
Then losing a bunch in the market.

Yea, my life's been pretty tough
And taken its toll
So I've got good reason
To have a face like a road map.

But other things come to mind
My mother's love,
Golfing with my father,
Telling stories to my brother

Camaraderie with my friends,
A faithful dog,
A warm and happy home,
Loving intimacy with my wife,

Being successful with my job,
Great fishing trips,
Fun picnics in the park,
Dinners with extended family,

I think I've got it figured out!
It wasn't all bad,
And looking at that face,
Some wrinkles were from the smiles!

PLUSES

I remember the day
When a store clerk said
"I gave you a Senior Discount."
That just about floored me.

Soon after that sad day
I got a card in the mail
That allowed me to join
An association of old people.

"Now wait a minute? I said.
"Why the heck did I get this?
I'm too young to need an outfit
To go lobby Congress for me!"

"And what's the deal here?
It says I get discounts on stuff
And cheap old folks insurance."
Like I need that or something!

Then somebody asked me
"Aren't you ready to retire?"
"When I'm darn good and ready!"
Was all I had to say.

And as far as Social Security
I worked hard for that,
And if I choose to draw it,
It's nothing to do with being old!

Then, at the local grocery store,
When I was on my way out
With a big load of groceries
A boy offered to help me with it.

"It is a little heavy" I said
"But I think I can make it."
My back hurt afterwards
But I still had my pride.

The same kind of thing happened
When I went to an office building.
I'm used to opening doors for others,
Now someone opened one for me.

"Do I look that frail?" I thought.
Just because that door was big
And I had to really tug on it.
But I woulda' gotten it open.

Then I sat down and I thought it out.
You know, discounts are kinda nice,
And that insurance would help,
And I don't like a hurting back.

And I reasoned I really did need
The income from the S.S. check,
And help with the door was OK.
People do seem to be nicer lately.

Besides, you're supposed to retire
When you're still able to enjoy it.
"So what the heck," I thought
"Getting old does have its pluses."

LIFE-FORCE

Our inner self stands in the back of our persona like green tree.
It is rooted deep in the rich earth of our former lives,
And draws its sustenance from the life-blood of our experiences.
It is fruitful or it is barren according to its season,
And according to the benevolence or drought of circumstance.
It is verdant always after dormancy,
With but a few dead branches here and there among the leaves
To tell the tale of a hard winter.

The tale of those branches says the season was bitter,
And was a time of drought of hope, non-generation of purpose,
And the pestilence-ridden consciousness which drives out love.
It was cold, and had nothing but the mechanics of half-used logic
To fill the void of darkness.

But on the now-green leaves is written another tale
Of deep roots and strong sap which will run with warmth
When the winds of hope, purpose, and love seek it out.
And when this three-fold zephyr engulfs its outstretched arms
Then there is a cry and a joy which rends the order of life,
And swells to take all of Now into a turmoil of feeling.

Then it falls into the resplendent silence of deeper truth
Which is like the eye of a hurricane,
And it stands there waiting with its energy circling.
And this free-flowing power never abates
But like the wind, springs up in gusts occasionally
And scatters its seeds into forever
With the incandescent glow of a Roman candle,
To be seen, recorded, remembered, and relived.

And that thing which we are really has grown and flourished,
And has spent another season sinking its taproot deeper
Into the well-spring of eternity.

ABOUT DENNIS BOURRET

Dennis Bourret is currently the music director for the Tucson Junior Strings, a national model program instilling leadership for creative and intelligent students of orchestral music. These young musicians perform without a conductor, and in so doing develop leadership, teamwork and a sense of musicality that goes way beyond the average orchestral experience. Dennis has instructed over six thousand public school age musicians over a span of forty-six consecutive years with the disciplines of technique and the art of creativity. What does all this have to do with poetry? Timing, lyricism, and sagacity are what Dennis brings to his poetry audience. Dennis also brings a unique perspective which drives his subject matter from the heart of America, through the jungles of Vietnam in wartime, through unique observations of daily life and finally to addressing the philosophical realms of existence.

Dennis was raised mostly in small towns in western Nebraska and Wyoming off Highway 20. He began playing the violin in elementary school and writing imaginatively while in junior high. Coming out of high school he had fully funded college scholarship offers in both journalism and music, ultimately choosing the music career path -but never dropping his pen throughout his life. In 1968, after completing three degrees in both violin and viola, Dennis was drafted into the United States Army and sent to Vietnam. There he spent half of his year directing howitzer fire while protecting a Special Forces patrol base on the Cambodian border. He endured being the target of daily enemy fire, the loss of close comrades, and being wounded by shrapnel on three separate occasions.

Upon release from his service, Dennis moved to Tucson, Arizona where he currently resides with his Tucson Junior Strings partner and wife, Anna. In their service to Tucson Junior Strings they have turned their pet project into a nationally recognized music education program that has been praised by some of the highest level musicians in the United States. In addition he has held principal chair positions in the Tucson Symphony, Arizona Opera Orchestra and Tucson Pops Orchestra. He also was a founding member of a professional piano quartet that toured internationally. Dennis also wields a baton and has been a guest conductor and clinician for high school honor orchestras and college festivals across the United States.

Made in the USA
Las Vegas, NV
30 September 2021

31422136R00074